T0028486

Text copyright © 2024 by Deborah Hodge
Illustrations copyright © 2024 by Karen Reczuch

All rights reserved. No part of this publication may be reproduced, stored in a retrieval system or transmitted, in any form or by any means, without the prior written consent of the publisher or a license from The Canadian Copyright Licensing Agency (Access Copyright). For an Access Copyright license, visit www.accesscopyright.ca or call toll free to 1-800-893-5777.

Published in 2024 by Groundwood Books / House of Anansi Press
groundwoodbooks.com

We gratefully acknowledge for their financial support of our publishing program the Canada Council for the Arts, the Ontario Arts Council and the Government of Canada.

With the participation of the Government of Canada
Avec la participation du gouvernement du Canada | Canadä

Library and Archives Canada Cataloguing in Publication
Title: West Coast wild rainforest / words by Deborah Hodge ; pictures by Karen Reczuch.
Names: Hodge, Deborah, author. | Reczuch, Karen, illustrator.
Series: West Coast wild series.
Description: Series statement: West Coast wild ; 4
Identifiers: Canadiana (print) 20230462405 | Canadiana (ebook) 20230462510 | ISBN 9781773068398 (hardcover) | ISBN 9781773068411 (EPUB) | ISBN 9781773068404 (Kindle)
Subjects: LCSH: Rain forest ecology—Pacific Coast (North America)—Juvenile literature. | LCSH: Rain forests—Pacific Coast (North America)—Juvenile literature.
Classification: LCC QH104.5.P32 H63 2024 | DDC j577.3409795—dc23

The illustrations were done in watercolor and color pencil.
Edited by Emma Sakamoto
Designed by Lucia Kim
Printed and bound in China

WEST
COAST
WILD
RAINFOREST

For my family, with love
— DH

For Bruce and Jude,
companions on the path
through the woods
— KR

WEST COAST WILD

RAINFOREST

WORDS BY

DEBORAH HODGE

PICTURES BY

KAREN RECZUCH

GROUNDWOOD BOOKS

HOUSE OF ANANSI PRESS

TORONTO / BERKELEY

Towering over the edge of the sea, along the
Pacific west coast, is an ancient and beautiful
rainforest. Mighty trees reach high into the sky.
Bountiful rain pours down on them, year after
year and century after century.

This lush green wilderness is home to a unique
community of plants and animals, thriving in an
interconnected web of life.

What will you find in this magnificent place?
Step into the rainforest and see.

Rain!

The rainforest is cool, rainy and foggy — and
one of the wettest non-tropical places on Earth!
Moisture-filled air coming off the ocean showers
it with more than ten feet (three meters) of
rain a year. The abundant rain keeps the forest
safe from fires, allowing the trees to grow for
hundreds of years. Some are as tall as a twenty-
storey building.

A Forest of Conifers

Most of the trees are conifers — trees that keep their leaves or needles in winter, and grow cones. Soft mosses and wispy lichens carpet their branches and trunks. Alongside the ancient trees are younger, smaller trees and seedlings beginning their life. Lush ferns and shrubs grow thick among them. The forest is a stunning mosaic of green!

A Forest Home

The rainforest provides shelter and food for many species. In return, many species give back to the forest. Douglas squirrels nest in trees and nibble on the seeds inside conifer cones. The squirrels also store cones under logs or in stumps to eat later. Some of the seeds from these cones will sprout and become new seedling trees.

Salmon Streams and Trees

Trees, young and old, shade the streams of the
rainforest and keep the water cool for the baby salmon
that hatch in the spring. At the edge of a stream, tree
roots hold the soil in place so that the water runs clean
and clear. The young fish spend several months here,
then swim to the ocean where they become adults.

The Cycle of Life

A few years later, in the fall, the adult salmon return to their streams to spawn. The females lay their eggs in the stream's gravel, and the males fertilize them. Afterwards, the adult salmon die, and their bodies are devoured by insects. The insects will be food for the baby salmon that hatch from the eggs next spring. New life begins from old!

Feeding the Forest

Bears, wolves and eagles feast on the spawning salmon. They carry their catch into the forest, eating the best parts of the fish, and leaving leftovers that decompose and fertilize the plants and trees. In this wonderful cycle of nature, the trees protect the salmon and the salmon feed the trees.

Black Bears

A black bear finds cover among the dense tangle of shrubs, ferns and berry bushes in the undergrowth and often makes its den in the hollow of a large tree. The bear's droppings, scattered after a salmon feast, add nutrients to the forest and enrich the plants and trees. A black bear may eat up to six hundred salmon a year!

Bald Eagles

These regal birds gather on the Pacific west coast, where they can build massive nests in the rainforest and feed on the plentiful salmon. Perched high in the trees, overlooking the ocean, an eagle can easily spot its prey and dive down at great speed to catch the salmon, sea birds and other small animals it hunts.

Gray Wolves

A mother wolf gives birth in a den, often under the roots of a big tree. The den and its underground tunnels keep her pups hidden and safe until they are old enough to travel with their pack. When the young wolves are ready, the adults will teach them how to fish for salmon and hunt for deer.

Black-Tailed Deer

Big eyes, sharp hearing and a keen sense of smell let a deer know when a hungry wolf or cougar is nearby. These graceful animals browse at the edges of the forest, feeding on plants, twigs, bark and berries. The plants they nibble beside a stream are full of nutrients added by salmon remains.

Western Screech-Owls

A tree cavity carved out by a woodpecker makes a good home for a screech owl. The cavity provides space and protection for the babies that will hatch there. During the day, the owl perches near its roost. At night, this stealthy hunter silently swoops down on mice, birds and other small forest animals, capturing them with its powerful talons.

Chestnut-Backed Chickadees

Flocks of tiny birds flit through the forest, singing brightly and foraging for insects in bark or along a branch. A mother chickadee makes a cozy nest for her babies in a small cavity, lining it with moss and lichens gathered from trees, and fur from deer or other animals.

Banana Slugs

The banana slug is the second largest slug in the world! It can grow as long as the yellow fruit it is named for. Its soft body is covered in thick slime that helps it glide along the forest floor. Banana slugs eat decaying plants and animals and recycle them into a rich waste material that fertilizes the soil and nourishes the rainforest.

The Forest Grows

When an old tree falls and decays, it becomes a "nursery log" that helps new trees grow. Drifting seeds from other trees sprout on top of it. Raised up by the log, the tiny seedlings catch the sun's light through a gap in the forest. The new little trees grow strong and tall, feeding on the log's nutrients and moisture.

The ancient rainforest at the edge of the Pacific Ocean is a rare and pristine wilderness, with a unique ecosystem that is linked in many ways.

The animals need the forest for food and shelter, and the plants and trees rely on the nourishment the creatures bring. Salmon are the key link, connecting the ocean and forest, and the plants and animals. When the salmon are abundant and healthy, the forest and all its inhabitants flourish.

THE PACIFIC WEST COAST RAINFOREST

Along the Pacific west coast, stretching from Alaska to Northern California, is a magnificent band of temperate rainforest with massive trees that are hundreds and perhaps even thousands of years old. These ancient giants include Sitka spruce, Western redcedar, Western hemlock and Douglas-fir — some of the largest trees in the world. Growing among them are younger, smaller trees and tiny seedlings. The coastal rainforest is a rich mix of ages, sizes and species!

The rainforest is temperate, with a cool climate year-round and an abundance of rain — more than ten feet (three meters) a year — making it one of the wettest non-tropical places on Earth. Most of the trees in the rainforest are coniferous, unlike tropical rainforests or temperate rainforests in other areas that have a higher proportion of deciduous trees.

Almost half of North America's coastal rainforest is found in British Columbia. In addition, the province holds nearly 25 percent of the remaining temperate coastal rainforests in the world.

The trunks and branches of the rainforest trees are lined with a soft carpet of bright green moss and long wispy lichens. Between the trees is a dense undergrowth of shrubs, ferns, fungi, berry bushes and more. This lush wilderness is home to a diverse community of species thriving in an interconnected web of life.

Eagles, bears, cougars and wolves share the forest with many other creatures that live in rivers and streams, on the forest floor or high in the branches of the tallest trees. The rainforest provides the animals with shelter and food, and the creatures, in turn, contribute to the healthy growth of the plants and trees, and one another.

For example, trees shade the forest streams, keeping the water cool for salmon eggs and babies. Later, after spawning salmon return from the ocean, they become an important food source for many creatures. Wolves, eagles and bears carry their salmon catches into the forest, leaving behind nutrient-rich remains that feed the trees.

The relationship between the salmon, ocean and forest is so significant that salmon are known as a "keystone species" — a species that many other species depend on. If the salmon are healthy, so is the entire ecosystem.

In the words of the Nuu-chah-nulth, who have lived as stewards of the land and sea on the Pacific west coast for thousands of years, "Everything is one and all is connected."

For decades, the logging of the ancient trees for lumber has been a contentious issue in British Columbia. Forestry companies continue to be at odds with those who wish to preserve the old-growth forests. Indigenous peoples, conservationists and other concerned citizens of every generation are actively protesting and working hard to protect this precious habitat.

Towering over the majestic Pacific Ocean, the west coast rainforest is a rare and beautiful place. It is an extraordinary wilderness that teems with life — and is vital to preserve.

For Further Exploration

Websites
"Coastal Rainforest." *Hinterland Who's Who.* Canadian Wildlife Federation, 2011. Online.

"Creature of the Month." *Pacific Rim National Park Reserve.* Parks Canada, 19 Nov 2022. Online.

"Great Bear Rainforest." *Vimeo*, uploaded by MacGillivray Freeman Films, 2022.

"Rainforest in Canada! Where?" *Pacific Rim National Park Reserve.* Parks Canada, 19 Nov. 2022. Online.

Books
Curious Kids Nature Guide: Explore the Amazing Outdoors of the Pacific Northwest. Cohen, Fiona, illustrations by Marni Fylling. Seattle: Little Bigfoot, 2017.

Nowhere Else on Earth: Standing Tall for the Great Bear Rainforest. Vernon, Caitlyn. Victoria: Orca Books, 2011.

Rainforest: Ancient Realm of the Pacific Northwest. Davis, Wade, photography by Graham Osborne. Vancouver: Greystone Books, 2000.

Salmon Creek. LeBox, Annette, illustrations by Karen Reczuch. Toronto: Groundwood Books, 2004.

West Coast Wild: A Nature Alphabet. Hodge, Deborah, illustrations by Karen Reczuch. Toronto: Groundwood Books, 2015.

Acknowledgments

Thank you to the many people who have made this book and the others in the series possible. I'm especially grateful to my lovely editor, Emma Sakamoto, my talented co-creator, Karen Reczuch, and our wonderful west coast expert and biologist, Adrienne Mason (writer and former managing editor of *Hakai Magazine*), who kindly reviewed the art and text for accuracy, and spent an amazing afternoon hiking in the rainforest with us. I would also like to express my sincere thanks to Michael Solomon, art director, and designer Lucia Kim for beautiful pages, and to Karen Li, publisher, and the entire Groundwood team for their support of us and work. Thank you, all!